Free Verse Editions

Edited by Jon Thompson

Blood Orbits

Ger Killeen

Parlor Press
West Lafayette, Indiana
www.parlorpress.com

Parlor Press LLC, West Lafayette, Indiana 47906

Printed in the United States of America
S A N: 2 5 4 - 8 8 7 9

Library of Congress Cataloging-in-Publication Data

Killeen, Ger, 1960-
  Blood orbits / Ger Killeen.
      p. cm. -- (Free verse editions)
  ISBN 978-1-60235-123-3 (pbk. : alk. paper) -- ISBN 978-1-
    60235-124-0 (adobe ebook)
  I. Title.
  PR6061.I35B56 2009
  821'.914--dc22

                                        2009032567

Cover art: Excavation I. Acrylic on Paper. © 2007 by Saba H.
    Qizilbash. Use by permission.
Printed on acid-free paper.

Parlor Press, LLC is an independent publisher of scholarly
and trade titles in print and multimedia formats. This book
is available in paper and Adobe eBook formats from Parlor
Press on the World Wide Web at http://www.parlorpress.
com or through online and brick-and-mortar bookstores.
For submission information or to find out about Parlor Press
publications, write to Parlor Press, 816 Robinson St., West
Lafayette, Indiana, 47906, or e-mail editor@parlorpress.com.

For Laoise and Sorcha Fitzgerald, Shazene Hussain,
and Hazel Fiedler

תּוֹחֶלֶת מְמֻשָּׁכָה, מַחֲלָה-לֵב;   וְעֵץ חַיִּים, תַּאֲוָה בָאָה.

Contents

Blood Orbits

Calendar

Now it is one era; now,
another. The sky
burns purple, unpronounceable;
the hours are a bristling
looped into your nerves.
And so, the rock-doves plunge and swoop;
sight strains to parse
their scattering into
verbs inflected for the future;
a hand like amber smoke casts
yarrow sticks, bundles them
promisingly; so many silvery cities
trilling in the solar winds.
Soon the oceanic clatter
of a talus slide;
soon the fluent stutter of guns.

The Abyss of the Birds

The hours flashed, flicked
their crests; I broke
through the scenery
to the eternal half-
smile of hooks:

I was a man
like a tree, walking.

Sparrows came in gusts,
cranes came, and hawks.
I held their cries; there was
a sound of leaves; I held them,
gave them back as smoke.

To the Counterglow

To the counterglow, to
the lesser darkness
barely shading
out from the greater,

follow the famine-
script limping across
the complicit plane
again and again. Against

a noctuary's
petering out in ashes
set one human carpal
sailing backwards

with a few willow baskets,
a few amphorae
for the next trial,
your's or another's.

The Translator's Dream

There are poppyseed cakes
cooling on the window sills,
there are horses swimming
in the rich grass beyond.

Towards evening, the sky
grows more primrose,
the mammulus clouds
yellow as a girl's hair:

indoors, the new light bleaches
all his spread-out papers blank.
And a rain that begins
as dashes turns into periods:

"*Es heißt 'virga'*", a stork
clacks from the loft.
Soon he can hear the roof
whine under the grainy weight,

see the land as far as the eye
can see take on a black gleam.
The postman knocks twice,
slides under the door a postcard

of Goethe's spreading oak:
"*I waited and waited.*
Why did you not come?"
in a hand he doesn't know,

and no return address.

Finisterre

Only the doggerel
of forgetting, bitten-off palatals
of Gaulish spat
out of baffled faces, crab-
crackle of carpals: it is
late; a whirring psalm salts itself
in between the embroiderd edges
of every scar combed across
the tableaux of unicorns and roses
massed on the endless
leveled lands behind. The sea
widens its blind eye. All
I want to know is
who sees this,
what has been hoped
asunder by wave after wave
of men in invisible ships?

Blood Orbits

(To Simone Weil)

Prayermower, periodic
comet.

Of the perennial verbs
nothing left

but the stalks.   You keep one
step ahead, out-

traveling the snowline,
the interrogation cell,

the gnomon's testscalpel.
You listen for silence

where the crowing calipers
browse on the zodiac.

You feed yourself
through the pummeled lips

one more night

First Flesh

Hand—terminal azimuth
hiving the new verbs of plenty:
cast, grasp, cup, rub between the fingers...
and so it is a pitched brightness,
part salt, part spilling, part
disappearance into some cut less
known than night which migrates
out of the pulsed breath that was
all you sensed of the other side
of the infinite margin.

Tenebrae

Hope-hours. A snowy hum
darkens through
the companionable chatter
hedging us off.

Poised heronlike above
the sense-rifts
your mouth zeros in on
a breath's hesitation.

I lie with you
in the unquotable instant
before a vowel, kiss
you out of hunger.

Twinberry

Ravenblack. Gleaming.
To eat is to become
speechless,
as though you are caught
in the seahiss
between transmissions.

The blue jay fanning
his blackish headcrest,
the smell of an alder
catkin, a face you love,
dissolve in the twilit
sibilance of the same word.

Once, early Summer,
each of the yellow
tubular flowers was the paired
node of a new phrasing,
a tenuous, exact rendering
of promise. Once.

To eat is to fall
somewhere like the inside
of a stone, gray and amniotic. Seahiss.
Without end.
Seahiss engorging
the lungs of myth.

Winged Book

(for Sandra Landers)

From somewhere beyond
the roiling origins of bone
and need, where all the oldest
hurts and breakages
root determinedly,
you wedge a blade of flame
in the impossibly thin
season between words: This,

then, how blessing can enter
the tumult of our days' lost
answers to hearts that plunge
along an arc of senseless
pain; this then how flight
is possible again beyond
reason, how blue exclamations
leap into joy, praise.

Figures and Grounds

1. Vendémiare

What begins as your heart wanting
to be heard
out, finally, beyond all
capricious arrayals
proves the devil to redo:

you step into the street
and find
you've accomplished
a kind of bolero over and above
the specific blessings
of freedom (search, seizure,
silencing, etc.) that coagulate
into magnets for good
sense, boutique art.

The other year, you unlocked,
let's say, some old alchemical emblem-
book, its tendons rubbed
raw by innumerable pressings, and you
couldn't resist adding
a pinch of your own dirt,
smartening it up
for the next performance
of *Vive L'Humanité*.

And what is it you see
in the other focus
of your elliptical flight
back from the republic of afar?
A well-appointed loft
in the fourteenth arrondissement,
a wife swallowing a sabre,
and taciturn daughters
with gold nipple-piercings,
lavish Ukiyo-e tattoos.

2. Brumaire

The storm discovers
its voice, and the meanings
multiply gust by gust.

It all becomes
a city of one dream. Think
of sleep as a fire

whose blown white heat
brings out layer
after smudged layer

of sentences
quilled in citron inks,
book chapters, perhaps.

The lucky salvage
fistfuls of smoke, pen
them away inside

the orbital cavities
sunk in lovely skulls. So many
eyes the color of parchment

perching like pigeons
on spires, on ramparts,
so many chilling nights

of hilarious weeping.

3. Frimaire

You are received, shown
in out of the night air.

Drawing room jammed with family
things: the walls hard-finished a shy blue,
the woodwork, blue, a rich carpet
of yellows, greens and blues in tendrils looping
through golden spaces, a large, round
mahogony table in the center of the room,
with a blue cloth on it, with a thin layer
of books in smart bindings, a tea-colored leather
sofa against one wall, against another
a row of four black walnut chairs
with horsehair seats, hung on a third,
between the street windows, a gilt mirror,
and, beneath, a black marble-topped
console table; also, a triangular stand
for china shepherdesses and farm animals;
also, on the walls, various prints
including peasants praying the Angelus,
and a still-life with lemons; a piano
strewn with sheet music for Field's *Nocturnes*,
a very tall clock from which on
the quarter hour issues an arresting
set of chimes and a flat figure
of Orpheus chasing a flat figure of Eurydice,
an enormous chandelier,
heavy ochre curtains and an open
fireplace with a white marble mantlepiece
against the chill.
                    A sumptuous
light mitres each and every

object nouns have shrivelled to a shadow of.
You, however, hypocrite voyeur,
are a spectral inconvenience in
the domestic schedule, (one alarming sickle
of the open-ended parentheses
between dinner-time and bedtime. The entire
ménage is worried for the safety
of the children because every sentence
addressed to you you repeat back
several times with very different
intonations, and your almost grimy
calling-card is hand-written with
milk me sugar in greenish ink.

That could spell the end
of your future presence
in the better houses.

4. Nivôse

To one a smoldering
coal, to the other
a mouthful of ash,
each and every one its own
hunger: pressure
enough to hold
the swell and hum,
the clatter tumbling over
the royal roads a night
or part of a night.

Otherwise
only rehearsed sayings
bunched up under
the teeth, fitful
squeaking as of
pipistrelles under eaves
steeply pitched against
the weight of articulacy
that is the sad
measure of days.

To one
a few true things,
to the other
a few more.
Otherwise
tragedy
and *farce*
and *tragedy*.
Without end.

5. Pluviôse

Something she thinks appeals
to the finest structures
of the ear-bones
the way a far-off train

with its packed casks
of cured fury precipitates
tundra, migration
routes, undeciphered

obelisks. Uncountable second
elements of the species
binomials of birds
are called after her. And a law

of sound mutation. The streets
lean in over her, canyons
after a flash flood
scours visible

all the strata
of sour sentences
and tight-lipped puzzlements
that drive the rest of us

to invent each other's
interior dialogs: *"She's not the one*
they'll come after",
Lily's husband says,

"you're the one
they'll come after.

And then", he says, "then,
where will we be? Eh?"

"But all I said", says Lily,
"is 'Don't take no for an answer,
luv'. S'not like I put 'er up to it."
"Mark my words", he says,

"It'll be your word
against 'er's."

6. Ventôse

1.

Words, part
turbulent
wind; weathersigns

casting their
unstrained pen-
umbrae. The sky tussles

flammable
balloons and their gondolas
rising off for

some sweet land.

2.

When was it
you first noticed
the over-

lap of geometry
and the ominous senses
in *"A windy day is not*

the day for thatching",
decoded the threats
by working through

the implications
of *thatch* and *text*?

3.

Look at the turns
of these centuries,
the places where

the proverbial
envectors
the logical;

look at the morning
reddening
its own unnavigable

wake.

7. Germinal

At the edges of the fields
(At the edges of real fields?)

the air trembles under
(the air trembles, a warped lens)

the inquisition of dust.
(contingency, fevers, bronze)

Fables of birth-stories
(porus as dreams, porus as hands)

riddle and sift
(sift and riddle)

the entire known world
(a fearful sphere, the letter Tau)

into forests and gardens.
(you and me, me and you)

The rivers talk past each other,
(silences translating badly, badly)

some rising up through helmet-horns,
(apparitions, coils of grievance)

some ferrying the rubble of symbols,
(mounds, mounds and ziggurats)

into the body of the missing,
(graph of mistimed leaps)

you and me, new arrivals.
(circumstance, spasm, wobble)

8. Floréal

Another morning's broken.
The early stun of imperious heat
bruises the smell out of
the rose trees so they unfold
another dimension of a war's radiance
at your floor-to-ceiling window.
                         Last night
the girl in green silks singing ghazals (*in the glow
of the almost randomly placed lamps
in the cooling courtyard where the officers
and their guests lounged and smoked and filled
the brass spittoons with crimson paan juice*)
was a shimmer as of someone calling
to you from under water. Even before
metaphor the rose she sang
was not a rose; the measure
of desire being the exotic
made familiar, a Hegelian
imbalance embodied, eroticized
in a chorus
*Kali kali zulfon ke phande nah dalo
Your long black hair has entangled me in its tresses*
                         You held her look
like a specimen in a cloudy jar, and she held
in a single note
reality and injustice that split you
from you that splits you
from you, made you stronger,
makes you richer.

9. Prairial

The mountained horizons retreating
retreating inside
your logbooks as you
decamp from sentence to sentence
on the way to   on the way to

Sunsets drip into
the waste of time,
(waste calling to emptiness
waste calling to vastness)
the lines spinning out
a tenuous sense of direction.

Some nights woken up
where a dream is hinging
back on the machinery of form all
the constellations slough off
the skin of signification
like a tree unleaved reveals
its adventitious branchings.

You doubt after that
anyone could return
to a country cottage or a town house
without caskets of plunder
or the physical proofs
and artifacts of miracles.

And so you go this way
and so you go that,
one choice turning
into another turning
into another

10. Messidor

Not unlike a philosopher
I can't say I
will stop at nothing: the sheer
lush goodness of the days,
your arms holding on to me
as we sleep, honey-
suckle at the open window,
has a way of wilting
so tormentingly I know
the temptation of wanting
to make up random
compensatory miracles.
                              Do you
know this sense of being
caught in a backwash,
tumbled endlessly in
the turbulence of some-
thing that explains without
being an explanation? Let's say
I put an adjective
like "lonely"
with a noun like "sky", make
up a formally plausible phrase
like "Sex for me is nothing
more than inserting myself
into someone's dream". Do you
think there is light here?
Or something dark? O cité,
who are you staring at
"like a dog with totally empty eyes";
O cité, as what do you present
yourself when I stare back?

11. Thermidor

I.

War-bleached or peace-bleached
the blonde beasts line
the coastline, purr inside the day's
tangerine webbing of prefabricated
inwardness. Two Mirage jets practice laying down
the coordinates of memory
on Mare Nostrum, overhead, while the young
women burn prayerful cigarettes for Saint
Trop, patron of proverbial weightlessness
and cut-and-paste erotica.

II.

Then it rains.
Then it's night.
Then the sky films

with an oil
of mythic litter
that won't mix

with your suspicions
about the meanings
of ordinary words.

Luckily, you have
the insomnia that extenuates
a doubtful identity,

and part of you
lulls the other parts
to a precarious sleep.

That's where you learn
to go poaching
a language more cloven

of reference, unfill
the silky gaps
where sunbathers make free

with contrails, rummage
in *The Fables of Aesop*
and your own diary.

III.

You wake up dangerous,
swimming in a zone of midnight-blue.
Eyeless voyeur!
Now you go this way,
now that,
now the other.

12. Fructidor

There is a place,
a place where elisions go, and hard,
hard to follow.

All around, all about, the pronouns,
edgy as cats, move and shake,
move and shake the sharp

meridians; and assonate,
and alliterate, and assonate loudly
with the huge echoes of

"last night"
"childhood"
"The Holy Roman Empire".

But there forms a place,
hard to go, where
elisions are, says *open*,

says *you pry open one door*
of a dense parenthesis: breath
from the orchards,

the migrant apple-pickers
from Oaxaca (from Oaxaca)
are digging a hole

for a blue baby, she's blue
this baby, in the hayfield. Corazón,
corazón, hard to follow,

but you know, now
you know how deep the place is
where elisions keep, how near.

And canto
means song, and canto
means the corner

of the eye.
Hard to follow, corazón,
hard to follow.

Approaching the Barricade

1.

Leicester Anjou Essex
spaces bound
into personage and
the endless sneer
of blood tinting the specific
lines that might other-
wise have drawn out
different ceremonies
tiny splendors
where even *The Faerie Queene*
is purged
in the acids of uncertainties
fere que...eque ne...far...eeee

2.

From the top
of that formidable pile
of cobbled virtues
precepts
absolutes   review
the parade of pain
one power after another
each banner a gap's
snapping camouflage
their names time-
bombs in the very bones
of thinking. Review that.

3.

under the weight of
under the flame of

a certain type of fabulous fact
might crack open when

the worst that could happen
continues to happen

might crack open by dint
of some wide

pronominal wedge
you and I together
with the forgotten
the half-forgotten ones

how we found
ourselves here.

Introduction to the Topography of Oregon

Beyond the pale the planes
of hills and riverbeds arrange
and rearrange themselves
unreliably; cattle-towns and mill-towns
orbit inside a nimbus of jumbled
plots like endless
rehearsals for the end of days.

M. Lewis might confide
in you a way of surviving
the unruliness of events
by scouting for marvels
among the drowned cairns' rubble,
attenuated glyphs of salmon:

float, hold
the breath, keep
the gaze turned down
as destiny buoys everything
up. And the things to be
hoped for: visions, ghost-dances,
fields of golden grain,
electricity too cheap to monitor.

In the Margin of the Anglo-Saxon Chronicle

Nettle-lauds
in the minster's scree,
speech bubbles hang
in the ice-core,
a wain to ride
back.
        A track
catastrophes made:
trails and paths
cross at unbelievable
angles. The figure of hope, an act
of faith in language
welding whales and stars.
Star-whale: recollection
of a lightning flash, clear
space
in solitary kennings.
The received wisdom is
far.

Land Grant

You fancy something lying
in wait for you from the other
side of the horizon
where, unnamed, for the moment, the mountains
drift, a rucked ribbon
of (how might you describe it?) linen,
off where the badlands
end. You resolve
to call your premonitions
sulphur buckwheat
and *prairie smoke*, the out-
ward, tempered facet your dreams
deploy, an unimaginative
but canny claim. It is all
so predictable when you look
back on it: this tedium
of a thousand brassy years
a sentence in whose threading
volutes you blur
into distant thunder,
you and yours; and so, kneeling
on a rug of entrails, you
give thanks for another day,
and another day, and another
unremarkable rape of the possible.

Hegelian Meditations

1. *The Cunning of Reason*

The buzz
of a proper noun being
awkwardly declined

down the hanging rope
ladder to the pit
of the locative

case closes in: Carpathia? Tree-rings
pulse out
in every direction

percussion
waves beyond
the oak posts

cart-horses used to
be tethered to past
half-spilt bags

of poppy seeds almost
germinating in puddles
of red. Your embroidered

shirt stained
with plum brandy
flew all the way

west and back
again east
carrying a boundary

in its breast
pocket with the whole
world scrolling out

marvellously legible
just where the trains
disappeared on the horizon.

2. *The Night of the World*

Now you lie in wait, waiting
beyond the TV's clearing
where the night arranges
itself into ripples
of reptilian vigor. Soon
you will slip into
the rheumy lagoons
of our moral luck
to drift among all
the little paper boats
with their guttering tealights.
What kind of hope is it
ferries you home on
the good ship ~~Rwanda~~,
the good ship ~~Darfur~~?

3. *Tarrying with the Negative*

Some granite-skinned thing
slips the leash of understanding,
goes for your fresh face;

the unhearable whistling its own

breath jets through your teeth
keeps it going
until you split:

in one of your eyes
glints a sprig of ice,
in the other, the lunar
half-gloss of a peeled apple.

We look back
at you and smile.

One Negative Way Of Looking At A Blackbird

After a time you give
up trying to hold

it all together—adieu
to those desperate

intercalations
at the Spring-gap's

ragged edge
that were keeping

a melody going,
keeping the thickets

tenanted. The new
burden, the middens

of feathers and claws,
encrypts silence

with what came before
silence, and you

must choose which you
prefer: the blackbird

actually singing
(which is false)

or the metaphor of the blackbird singing
(which isn't true).

Erebus and *Terror*

1. An Excellent Observation
of the Sun in Quicksilver

Home, sweetness of rotting tubers, eyes impaired in upwardness, civilized speeches ending in cucumber sandwiches and the exclamation points of musket-fire. What is the opposite of *Ahoy!* ? A foreign habitation where no one knows my name. There you are. Call me _____. Call me anything but back. People born with boots in their mouths know early on that transparency is the trick writing plays on confession. The lure of the lore of icebergs on a fine day slicing the parallels. It puts one in mind of the Castle Perilous. Don't answer that. Betray nothing. Nod and gape.

2. Comparing the Merits
of the Two Routes

Do maps have a point of view that wobbles with the maker? The context is television. Soon it will dawn Columbus Day in Heaven and precipitation will dilute the pastoral sophistries of summer with bluesy ring-tones. Is that really snow or is it confetti made from the shredded leaves of the National White Pages? Hunger is a good glass for the texture of things you'll confront in the clots of spacetime north of where the names end, where only the Esquimaux know how to eat the scenery. The Nullarbor Plain, so called because there is no harbor where a ship can put in, is, nonetheless, abundant in Uranium which is, with the proper preparation, nutritious and palatable. Men spend many years toughening themselves up for the promise-laden miles.

3. In England There Is Nothing New

The forensic stitchings of spikey syllogisms, the piecework of parliamentary business. Then tea. Black spores spatter the clotted cream. Outside the windows in the sour docklands clogged with the half-lost, they are savaging our language with their grotesque syntax. One of the monuments of mercy would be elocution. Then might the very sounds raise up these countenances, lurid and wintry and long. Then might they understand how much depends on whether verbs come before or after the subject, how great accomplishments stand or fall by such small and precious things.

4. Hereabout the Larch Trees End

What will we do without wood? In my voice I carry leaves clawed out of Cambrian caves. Is this a kaddish for oaks? Are these orisons for pit ponies? The antiphon of the engines chews out a palatial fantasy for starry generations to come after. In this idiom the word "yesterday" is only used in contexts of inevitability: See under *tomorrow*, see under *nuclear fusion*, see under *colonies of Mars*. And when the Red Sea opens a passage you discover if you're a chosen one or a charioteer in Pharaoh's army.

5. One Small Repeating Reflecting Circle

That silent film sparks tensions because no one remembers posing for the camera but everyone remembers being the director. In my picture you're greener than the breezeless sea and your mouth pulses, palatalizing and unpalatalizing a very unremarkable consonant. Civilized people want to laugh, but they know the gravity of it all, the observation of these breathing-holes in the pack-ice: a seal might feed you for days; otherwise you might have to swallow your leather boots. A colorful race, but totally untrustworthy, even the converts. Good material, strong backs, take orders well as long as there's a whip in the background. I love how the moon grazes and occults these stars. I love how it's only a figure of speech.

6. Reasons for My Engaging Hope as a Steersman

The Esquimaux have their shamans, the Kabloonas their spirit rappers for such sicknesses as arise from a wandering soul. Miss Maggie Fox transmits the tedious ramblings of the dead from her home in Rochester, the Styx bubbling up from between her lovely toes. Some nights we are pelted by artifacts launched out of our own cramped fantasy space to ripple and disappear in the mumbling pools of our inner lives. A gold watch. A scrap of embroidery. A surgeon's blade. The good names of Englishmen who devoured Englishmen by the banks of the Great Fish River break over our hearts in a drowning wave. Mr. Dickens casts us the rope of a saving sentence spun from the entrails of barbarous others. *A domesticity of blood and blubber.* All the furniture of my house is rattling and snapping like teeth.

7. The Coruscation Reassumed the Horseshoe Form

I inherit flagrancy from a long line of exceptionalists. Then I perceive how the limits of the possible flip into the limits of the probable and all the metaphors stink with abscesses in the joints. The wave equation of "virgin lands" collapses into serpentine leads in the pack-ice. We have no news. The comparative form of "lost" turns out to be "peripheral", the superlative "vestigial". By this time the men have taken to striking up a sea chantey called *The Reprisals of the Real*, weeping into their watered-down rum, playing endless hands of strip-whist with the phantasies they eloped with. I no longer even know what desire it is ignites me like the sky.

8. Numerous Stone Marks and Several Caches

Space is always a stand-in for time, glyphs and pictures the first line of defense against the disorders of memory. Five loaves and two fishes; a fatted calf; the ambivalence of things seen. The problem is that everything half-works until policy precipitates a famine. Suddenly, then, the kitschy cladding falls away from the engine of history and you hear the gearwheels of power recalibrating bounty. Providence, Providence, Providence. Empire's fire and Peel's brimstone. Perhaps I fled here to mark the progress of a disease, those middle voices that sequester the middle passage in pious ejaculations. After all, ich am of Irlaunde: in the chill and stupor of truths we toast Her Majesty with bumpers of paranoia and bile, bestow names like salt.

9. Beyond the Floating Light

I'm trying to recall how far out to sea in you I've been, the voyages from which I returned less than before I set out. The ghost of a chance looms in the margins, in the wings. A dead girl from the middle classes, wan and weary, apparates with a message and a map of Prince Regent Inlet. (That should have been a giveaway— the Dickensian staging, the candlelit sincerity, the unmissable subtext, viz. "*You* might be a high-and-mighty mucky-muck but *we* know where your *jouissance* lies, beggin' yer pardon, ma'am"). The jurisdiction of Victoria bites at her grave. Albion yearns through my letters. The sun never sets and we want more.

10. The Translation of Her Indian Name Is Burnt Weed

At the flung end of this signifying chain a smudge of milkthistle tests the unblinking space, crosses over into a dream's interregnum between chaos and terror. We're only interested in the phonemes of the fuckable ones we'll teach to read aloud *A Winter's Tale*. We bundle against the flensing edges of aurorae in skins of recruited idylls. They interpret *love* as *meat*, you know. *Nel mezzo del camin'* we scribble each other into mutually unmappable histories by the sheer sheen of seal-light, twist in the wind that shakes the sun and the other stars.

11. The Shingly Point of which I Have Spoken

Suppose, then, my letter arrives, grimed with guts, a pathetic footnote of the unhappy consciousness. Most want the engine to stop, the ship to coast to anchor in the lovely sweep of a bay in the hot Marquesas, to expel in an accomplishing breath the last nasal hum of *The Book of Revelations* or the final Sura of *The Holy Qu'ran*. Panton. Taww<u>a</u>ban. I always thought I was somewhere else because my narrative was ever accompanied by the uncanny music of slippages. We shared a bowl of warm seal blood. Since then I keep having visions of a shimmering periodic sentence with an indefinitely postboned principal verb. I wanted to write the prayer that begins "Give me a cheerful mind to perform your wonders..." All I got down was *riverrun*

Light Keeper

Say he comes out of nowhere with saltflakes
in his beard, nowhere far from
the Copernican provinces, peering out
from beneath the slick, misshapen caul
of 1900, skilled
in the ways of boats,
a canny reader of cloudshapes, diligent
polisher of concave mirrors:

I am unravelled back
by magnesium pulses
phrased in Morse and hollowed voices
from a wireless blooming and fading
in the unmetaphorical aether,
the name *Lusitania* unmoored
from what it tries to signify
opening a sensible tear

in the forecast weather;
with his eyes I look through
the night, deep through the scattered
galactic incandescence,
decode the Dog Star's mysteries
to an endless line of the ruined and lost.
He blows through a tunnel
of possibilities, blinded by his own ashes,

an afterimage branded
on his retina: a ruby
counterglow from the mud-colored future:
Gallipoli, the Somme.

September 1914

The motherlands circle.
With their long needles they begin
to quilt swaths of mushroom-
pale fog to the firmament,
making men of them. *Ave*,
sings the lark at dawn,
ave. Boys awake fascinated
by their newly minted trigger-
fingers, take them in their mouths,
the red nipples of a first love. Hearts
swing like censers, spilling
khaki-colored clouds in perfect time
with the tocsin-bells of Notre Dame.
Ave, sings the lark at dawn,
ave. No one even dreams
of inflecting it as a question. Such
a lovely September, weatherwise.
And then the Holy Ghost descends
in blue tongues of steel. *Ave. Ave.*

Gallipoli

We were so close
to Troy I could hear
bits of Ionic in the chatter
of a machine gun
as soon as the great orange
bird of the morning
rose from among
the imagined islands
to perch on the shoulders
of this man or that
of The Royal Munster Fusiliers.

The way a dream snakes
all through your body
to come out in
a swollen context,
so were the inaccessible
ridges inscribed by
an alphabet of beach-heads
spangling a wound
as metaphysical as
it was gangrenous. And I,
so blinded

by the boneshine,
kept my head
down in the spattered pages
of a School's Classic. Nothing
to relate
of the land
or accounts of comrades
except
Ἐλυθες εκ πολέμου
ως ώφελες ολέσθαι αυτοθι...
which is how Homer managed

to get through the slaughter.
Even what comes back
doesn't come back,
the sun, say, or the tides:
One phlegm of near-speech
displaced by another
that erases it; as if
everything is happening
for the first time.

Letters From The Front, 1906 – 2006

What can't be told
is frayed contexts
which ink bleeds

into, tying
our cropped
apostrophes one

to another. The plots
are so thin
you can hear

all the bones
under the reports.
At the height

of the chatterstorm
your grandfather
unroped himself

from the stake
of anthem, reached
through the acid

strata for your small
fingers. Now, on the eve
of the last

big push every home
in the motherland
stocks up on ice.

Jocasta

World history. The olives
rot in the groves. Children fall
asleep never to wake. My dreams
seep into my milk
that stinks of goats, sour wine.

Now you'll want explanations.
Now you'll want the whole
philosophical cry
of relief that issues
in the word *destiny*; you'll want
the choral platitudes
about the end being
coded inside the beginning
from the beginning, won't you?
Rise and fall. Strophe and antistrophe.
You'll want all that.

The roads open and cross
each other. Men unsheath
their arbitrary resentments.
There's death. There's copulation
and plunder, women tearing
boys asunder on the hills
above the city. Prayers
and singing and shrieking
to drown out
the unrelenting snigger
of *chance, chance, chance.*
What about that?

But you'll believe
anything. My husband
believes he's my son. The whole
country believes in
guilt and sacrifice
and redemption. World history.
When you wake up
terrified and falling
a text catches
you like a net
suspended
from generation to generation
over absolutely nothing.

Tree Alphabet

A marginal mention
an echo   of bearings
how to mind them   and lose them
senses entered
                    as an arbor where
the aspen consorts
with the beech
the cedar
with the dogwood   or perhaps
it's the ash   now
with the birch.

Listen how Prospero
tells Miranda
I would transfuse
thy blood with sap
thy sap with ink
thy ink with blood
and tell me   you don't
know   the same serene
discontentment you
feel on first   waking
you first felt
on first hearing
your first   story
how   as a child you went
        missing
refused to come back.

Gallia

The teacher, a Christian
Brother, his entire life
yellowed by tobacco
and prayers, assigns our weekend
translation passage
from *De Bello Gallico*.

No one that age
should be that happy
to give up a Saturday
in Spring for the severe
clarity of a soldier's
prose, an unspoken language.

A bedroom window overlooking
a province of coal-
smoke and venial sins,
a perpetual teatime,
hushed lusts, suburban
imprecations.

Rumours of all-
out war in the North,
a forensic rumbling—
*militia, prorogue,
security*. Another
script, another

story:
to an origin,
where Caesar deploys
his sentences against
the vast unreason
of the barbarous tribes.

I
watch
 my hand
glove itself
 in the very hand
of shaping power,

a traitor by metaphor,
scouting the lay of my own
land: *In the twilight he saw a fleet*
of luminous coffins come in
with the tide from the ragged margins
of yesterday and tomorrow.

Shannon Mercury

I.

Nimblest of fingers turning
down the volume of the fossil-
beds, your password
into brandname smiling
always a nod.

Under foot
Milesian, Danaan, equally
twitch their barbed probosces,
root around among mouth-holes
for certain truffles

as sulphuric acid might snake
through a timescape
past *faith an' begorrah*, past *integrated circuit*
to the marbled discounties
of Limerick, Kerry, Clare.

II.

Let's meet at the fabled ford
where St. Munchin's SUV
drove across the top of the water
to deliver a hamper of pirated DVDs
to fifty-thousand restless obese.
We can choose our weapons
from among a depleted-uranium-tipped gae bolgae,
a Quranic shoulder-fired missile-scimitar,
a pocket Ninja pulse-laser, and several

strains of aerosolized doom viruses.
Winner take all, and all will be well:
the professors of history will be
nanomachines coded to prove
the inevitability of you and yours
by modifying all data on the molecular level,
producing a genealogy with all supporting
landscapes, papyri, stelae, grave goods,
documents, sound recordings, films and genomes.
And who is to say you're not the instrument
of God, found in a hollow by the Shannon Pot,
wrapped in a space-blanket and laid
in an incubator at the Mater Hospital?
Stranger things have happened.

III.

As What's-his-name said:
"language is fossil murder";
and as the Other-fella then asked:
"Did that word-play of mine send out
Certain men the Americans bought?"
Well, if you accept the premise,
the answer is "without a doubt".
A poll commissioned for the *Shannon Mercury*
shows a consensus on this matter
among those who don't know any better.

IV.

Finally, to the necessary
quaternity: For as long
as mercury flows in the River Shannon

between the rocks of Curraghgower
my people will speak their native
silence with that lovely accent
formerly known as a *brogue*
but now called a *Nike*
in the East Timor suburb of Lower Drumcondra
where it breathes its first and last.
It's the tongue we dream in, me boyos,
full of the grace of uncomplicated assent
to what is over and done with.
The faces we had before our parents were born
appear to us nightly in dreams, rising
like moons with the coolest of confident smirks,
our likeness imprinted on earth, water, air and holy fire.
You know who we are.

Sea of Cortez

Azures and papaya
greens for the real
estate brochures,

and murder, coded
into the very sounds
of the colors,

descants on the fictive
anthems: Ours is
a potent confluence

of will and luck, theirs
a masticating allegory
of early and later.

The headlands
and the bays shrivel
in the shrinkwrap

of Castillian—
in spite of appearances
this one name is darkness

without a heart,
a stiletto that slips
between the eye and

its socket until
San This or San That,
burnished gold

by devotion
grants you visions
of floating cities

arriving with waltz music
through the heat haze,
the word haze.

A Shelter in Copan

An afternoon the color
of chocolate thunder.
Unchanging axioms
over ceiba trees radiant with rain.

Under
a palm thatch shelter that shades
a dynastic stela,
the idiom of royal notaries;

around me, the moat of lineage
ripples with half-lit syllables
still trying to conjugate
power with a kind of providence;

and might not a certain kind of pain
turn itself into vision?
A kneeling chieftan draws a cord
of stingray spines through a hole in his tongue,

and when the blood that drips down
has soaked strips of paper
that line a stone bowl on the ground
he mixes the paper

with aromatic plants
and sets it all alight to carry
the incense of his petitions
upwards to the gods

who appear with their answers:
The world lives on the raw edge
of an ever-fresh wound; which will you be,
the face ennobling the stone,

the rubble that holds it in place?

Ulisse

After the flame comes
to a place and time where my guide
believes us safe enough, he accosts it with:
"Listen, you two who are jailed in a single fire;
if for any reason you thought well of me
when I was writing my imperial myth,
stay here a moment and let the one of you
tell where he went to lose himself."
And the bigger blade of the ancient flame
starts to shake a murmuring out of itself
just like a flame that struggles in the wind;
then, lashing the top of itself this way and that,
as if it is a tongue that's forming sounds,
projects its voice outwards and speaks:
"When I left Circe, who kept me for
over a year near Gaeta (that's what the place is
called since Aeneas renamed it),
not a single human duty or fear
could quench the thirst I had inside me
to know the world and all its ways:
I struck out into the deep, open sea
with just a single ship and the small crew
who had not abandoned me.
Europe's coast, the coast of Africa,
I saw them both, yes, Spain and Morocco,
and Sardinia and all the other islands that sea breaks against.
My comrades and I had aged and slowed down
when we reached the narrow passage
where Hercules planted his sacred pillars
to warn off human beings from going farther.
On the right hand I passed beyond Seville,
on the left, had already left Ceuta in my wake.

'Brothers', I said, 'you have come through
a hundred thousand dangers to get this far West;
so, don't *now* close off your still-alive and alert senses
from the experience
of the tribeless world behind the sun.
Think of your origins! You weren't made
to exist like automata, but to search
out the deep meaning of things.'
With this brief speech I made my comrades
so eager for the rest of the journey
there was no holding them back.
And, turning the stern towards the dawn,
we turned our oars into wings for that wild flight,
always gaining on the left.
All the stars of the other pole rose
as night came on, and our own familiar stars
sank below the ocean floor.
Five times the moon had gone through all
its phases since we first set out
on our dangerous voyage, when,
there in the distance, dark and unbelievably huge,
loomed a mountain. We were ecstatic
to see it, but instantly from this new world
a storm blew up and struck our ship
head-on. Three times it spun us round
with all the waves then pitched us
vertical so gravity took hold
and the waters closed over our heads."
Then the flame goes still
and says no more...

*(A rewriting of Dante, Inferno,
Canto XXVI, 76-142, and Canto XVII, 1-2)*

Paula/Paul/Frank/Frances

So dark, so early this far
north. We walk soberly home

from the Academia Antiqva
Mvri Hadriani.

All along the avenues the keepers
of shoe shops and vegetable stands,

the owners of hardware stores
and the newsagents

pace and nod like sentries, exchange
weathertalk and goods

as though there were no
yesterday. Mirabile dictu

they believe we believe
in the limits of elocution

and grammar, an order beatified
by phonetic rightness. We are

good at school; we are good.
So when we study

each other's bodies we are
less undressed

than unvestmented, and the raw
nerves of our vernacular fire

scintilli... nuvoli... respiri
half-lit by a smudge of moon

like sparks in breathclouds
in the exquisite cold

of a town park's evergreens
by a town park's wall

fuck and finger-fuck
words unfurling objects

into wide open spaces
on a star-chart's verso

the wind on our skins
the salt of us

opening a current
out of a mouth

out of a harbor.

Influenza

Night. The spring sky. He writes *Stray pocks and rifts
of light scavenging among the blackness.* He writes
*vague outlines of alders down by the creek
crackling with the desperate exchanges of frogs.*

He'll need the italics later.

Sometime between Good Friday and Easter Sunday
the chatty owner of the little espresso hut
where he buys his mochas on the way to work
killed himself. He writes *On Spy Wednesday he served
me coffee. I was sniffling because of all
the tree pollen in the air, my eyes were running.
He asked me if I had the flu.*

This is where he pretends events rhyme.

Influenza comes from the Italian word
meaning "influence", specifically *the influence
of the stars on earthly affairs.*

He writes *Night. The spring sky.* He writes
Stars, stars, stars, stars. He writes *The sky is scarred
with the afterburn of other people's terrible certainties.*

Night. The spring sky. The tree frogs call all along the creek.

Surety, Part A

Are you certain there isn't a way in abbreviation? Are you certain there isn't a sign in an abdomen? Are you certain there isn't an island in abeyance? Are you certain there isn't an ego in abjection? Are you certain there isn't gold in aborigines? Are you certain there isn't a father in abracadabra? Are you certain there isn't a transgression in absinthe? Are you certain there isn't a sun in absolution? Are you certain there isn't a sea-voyage in absolve? Are you certain there isn't a sphere in absorbtion? Are you certain there isn't a metal in abstinence? Are you certain there isn't drama in abstraction? Are you certain there isn't an origin in absurdity? Are you certain there isn't a wave in abundance? Are you certain there isn't history in acceleration? Are you certain there isn't cash in an accent? Are you certain there isn't filth in accession? Are you certain there aren't teeth in an accident? Are you certain there isn't a mollusc in an acclamation? Are you certain there isn't a fizz in an accolade? Are you certain there isn't a rope in accordance? Are you certain there isn't a street in accrue? Are you certain there isn't a mother in achievement? Are you certain there isn't gunfire in acknowledging? Are you certain there isn't an edge in acrimony? Are you certain there isn't theft in acrobatics? Are you certain there isn't quaternity in activity? Are you certain there isn't an Egyptian god in adaptability? Are you certain there isn't anger in admiration? Are you certain there isn't a vehicle in advancement? Are you certain there isn't wind in adventure? Are you certain there isn't poetry in adversity? Are you certain there isn't Springtime in advertising? Are you certain there isn't shit in advocacy? Are you certain there isn't a mystic in an aerie? Are you certain there isn't an end in affinity? Are you certain there isn't music in an aftermath? Are you certain there isn't earliness in agony? Are you certain there isn't a revolutionary in alchemy? Are you certain there isn't a fish in alcohol? Are you certain there isn't surety in alienation? Are you certain there isn't timber in alignment? Are you certain there isn't recurrence in alliteration? Are you certain there isn't a slash in allocution? Are you certain there isn't pallor in allowance? Are you certain there isn't a game in alluding? Are you certain there isn't a toilet in aloofness? Are you certain there isn't a thigh in amalgamation? Are you certain there isn't nakedness in amanuensis? Are you certain there isn't a buddy in an amateur? Are you certain there isn't a low sound in ambassador? Are you certain there isn't China in ambiguousness? Are you certain there isn't liquor in ambivalence? Are you certain there isn't a bone in ambrosia? Are you certain there isn't shist in amicability? Are you certain there isn't a singularity in ammunition? Are you certain there isn't a current in amplitude? Are you certain there isn't a whore in amputation? Are you certain there isn't stubborness in an amulet? Are you certain there isn't sperm in amusement? Are you certain there isn't captivity in Anabaptism? Are you certain there isn't an old horse in an anagram? Are you certain there isn't a trajectory in anarchism? Are you certain there isn't definiteness in anathema? Are you certain there isn't indivisibility in anatomy? Are you certain there isn't rugby in ancestry? Are you certain there isn't prayer in Anchorage? Are you certain there isn't stickiness in angels? Are you certain there isn't cleverness in Anglicanism? Are you certain there isn't a blast in angustation? Are you certain there isn't Gaelic in anniversary? Are you certain there isn't negation in annotation? Are you certain there isn't weight in announcements? Are you certain there isn't royalty in anorexia? Are you certain there isn't humanity in answers? Are you certain there isn't a label in antagonism? Are you certain there isn't a twitch in antarctic? Are you certain there isn't pork in an antechamber? Are you certain there aren't others in an anthem? Are you certain there isn't choice in an aorta? Are you certain there isn't pain in Apache? Are you certain there isn't little in Apocalypse? Are you certain there isn't hatred in apodictic? Are you certain there isn't horseplay in apologies? Are you certain there isn't mail in apostasy? Are you certain there isn't a carriage in apostolic? Are you certain there isn't peeling in apparel? Are you certain there isn't tolling in appealing? Are you certain there isn't fruit in an appearance? Are you certain there isn't skin in an appellation? Are you certain there isn't cream in an appointment? Are you certain there isn't a chicken in apprehension? Are you certain there isn't allure in apprenticeship? Are you certain there aren't vermin in approaches? Are you certain there isn't an ellipse in approval? Are you certain there isn't reflexivity in an apse? Are you certain there isn't a drill in arbitration? Are you certain there isn't endearment in archery? Are you certain there isn't an onion in an archive? Are you certain there isn't lordship in Ariel? Are you certain there isn't weaponry in Armageddon? Are you certain there isn't an angel in arrangements? Are you certain there isn't a riverbank in arrivals? Are you certain there isn't a glove in arrogant? Are you certain there isn't a cry in arrowhead? Are you certain there isn't art in arson? Are you certain there isn't an arse in articulation? Are you certain there isn't being in ascension? Are you certain there isn't an odor in ascent? Are you certain there aren't women in the ashes? Are you certain there isn't venom in an aspect? Are you certain there isn't a British regiment in assassins? Are you certain there isn't a state in assignation? Are you certain there isn't honey in assimilation? Are you certain there isn't grease in assuetude? Are you certain there isn't a pump in assumption? Are you certain there isn't danger in an asterisk? Are you certain there isn't snobbery in astonishment? Are you certain there isn't a marriage in astringency? Are you certain there isn't a conditional in astuteness? Are you certain there isn't lifting in asymptotes? Are you certain there isn't a toll in ataxia? Are you certain there isn't iron in atheism? Are you certain there isn't a mythic bird in atrocity? Are you certain there isn't a reward in atrophy? Are you certain there isn't a cattle-raid in attainment? Are you certain there isn't a bivouac in attention? Are you certain there isn't a book in attraction? Are you certain there isn't a tribe in an attribute? Are you certain there isn't a cask in attunement? Are you certain there isn't a game in the audible? Are you certain there aren't cloves in auspices? Are you certain there isn't a hammer in authority? Are you certain there isn't a reversal in autopsy? Are you certain there aren't wools in autumn? Are you certain there isn't grain in avarice? Are you certain there isn't a wildflower in avenge? Are you certain there aren't battles in awards? Are you certain there isn't usage in azure? Are you certain? Are you certain? Are you certain?

Thoughts From A Garden

The hour darkens favorably.
May it be that fiery
groundsel, sword vetch
defect from this plot
walled by friezes of luminous
nostalgias. Absence makes
meaning meander,
a sap-acid eating
its way out of symbol
like the miraculous tears
of an icon erasing
the eyes they slide from.

On the outside
edges, in the supressed
collisions between the arclighted
intervals, the fictive
weeds of the future
uncurl in the overripe smoke,
begin their obscure push.

Fabulous the time which is
alive, again.

Notes

Figures and Grounds. The titles of the poems in this sequence are the names of the months in the French Revolutionary Calendar. Officially adopted in France on October 24, 1793 and abolished on 1 January 1806 by Emperor Napoleon I, it was used again briefly during the Paris Commune in 1871. The calendar was adopted a year after the advent of the First Republic (there was no year 1), after a long debate involving the mathematicians Romme and Monge, the poets Chénier and Fabre d' Eglantine and the painter David. The mathematicians contributed equal month division, and a decimal measure of time. The poets contributed the names of the days, choosing the names of plants, domestic animals and tools; the months rhyme three by three, according to the "sonority" of the seasons.

Erebus and Terror. 'Erebus' and 'Terror' were the names of the ships which the British explorer Sir John Franklin took to the Arctic in 1845 in an ill-fated attempt to find the Northwest Passage. 1845 also marked the beginning of the Great Irish Famine which was pushed off the front pages of the British press by breathless accounts of the Franklin voyage. The titles of these prose poems are taken from sentences in the journals which Franklin kept on an earlier expedition, and from sentences in the journals of John Rae who eventually found the remains of Franklin's ships. Rae discovered clear evidence of cannibalism among the crew, and on revealing his findings he was excoriated in the press by, among many others, Charles Dickens.

Gallipoli. The Greek is from Homer's *Illiad*, Bk. 3, line 428: "You have come from war: would that it had been your fate to have perished there".

Acknowledgments

I wish to thank the editors of the following publications in which versions of some of these poems have appeared:

Green Integer Review
Free Verse
Knockout
The Gertrude Stein Awards 2006

About the Author

Ger Killeen teaches in the Department of English and Writing at Marylhurst University near Portland, Oregon. His special interests are postmodern poetry, Celtic literature, the poetry of mysticism, and critical theory. He is the author of several books, including *A Stone That Will Leap Over The Waves* (Trask House, 1999), *A Wren* (Bluestem Press, winner of the Bluestem Award for Poetry), and *Signs Following* (Parlor Press, 2005).

His work also appears in several anthologies, including *From Here We Speak* (Ohio State University Press), *American Poetry: The Next Generation* (Carnegie-Mellon University Press), and *The Gertrude Stein Awards 2006* (Green Integer).

Free Verse Editions

Edited by Jon Thompson

2009

Divination Machine by F. Daniel Rzicznek
Blood Orbits by Ger Killeen
Under the Quick by Molly Bendall
Poem from above the Hill & Selected Work by Ashur Etwebi, translated by Brenda Hillman and Diallah Haidar

2008

Quarry by Carolyn Guinzio
Between the Twilight and the Sky by Jennie Neighbors
The Prison Poems by Miguel Hernández,
    translated by Michael Smith
remanence by Boyer Rickel
What Stillness Illuminated by Yermiyahu Ahron Taub

2007

Child in the Road by Cindy Savett
Verge by Morgan Lucas Schuldt
The Flying House by Dawn-Michelle Baude

2006

Physis by Nicolas Pesque, translated by Cole Swensen
Puppet Wardrobe by Daniel Tiffany
These Beautiful Limits by Thomas Lisk
The Wash by Adam Clay

2005

A Map of Faring by Peter Riley
Signs Following by Ger Killeen
Winter Journey [Viaggio d'inverno] by Attilio Bertolucci,
    translated by Nicholas Benson

www.ingramcontent.com/pod-product-compliance
Lightning Source LLC
Chambersburg PA
CBHW032027090426
42741CB00006B/753